Mexico Today

Contents

This picture shows the Plaza of the Three Cultures in Mexico City.
You can see old and new buildings there.

The green stripe in Mexico's flag means hope.
The white one means being clean.
The red one stands for the blood lost in war.

These fishermen are using fishing nets.
They are called butterfly nets.
Can you guess why they have that name?

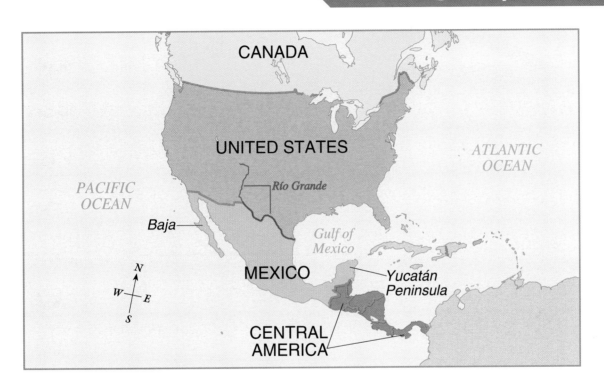

CANADA

UNITED STATES

ATLANTIC
OCEAN

PACIFIC
OCEAN

Río Grande

Baja

Gulf of
Mexico

MEXICO

Yucatán
Peninsula

N
W   E
S

CENTRAL
AMERICA

This map shows North America.
Mexico is the country that is colored green.

This picture shows part of the border between the United States and Mexico.

Chichén Itzá is an old Mexican city.
The Maya saw stars from this tower at night.

This volcano's nickname is Popo.
The name means "smoking mountain."

The rich soil of the altiplano is good for growing crops.
Many people live in this part of Mexico.

Families in Mexico celebrate important holidays together.
These families celebrate the Day of the Dead.

Christmas is a very special holiday in Mexico.
These children are telling the Christmas story.

This is Miguel Hidalgo y Costilla.
He helped Mexico become free from Spain.

Another Mexican holiday is Cinco de Mayo.
These words mean "the fifth of May."
Children dance and march in parades.

This market is in the town center.
People come here to buy and sell things.

This Mexican woman makes tortillas.
She takes dough and pats it flat.
She bakes tortillas for her family to eat.

This picture shows a mariachi band.
The members are dressed in fancy clothes.
What instruments do you see?